365

Writing

Prompts

ONE YEAR OF IDEAS TO GET YOUR B2B BLOG GOING

RICK RAMOS

Published by Rick Ramos Consulting, New York, New York 10001.

This publication is designed to provide accurate and authoritative information in regard to the subject matter covered. It is sold with the understanding that the publisher is not engaged in rendering legal, accounting, or other professional services. If legal advice or other expert assistance is required, the services of a competent professional person should be sought.

Questions for the author?
rick@rickramos.com
www.rickramos.com

About the Author

Mr. Rick Ramos is a seasoned veteran in online marketing with over seventeen years' experience developing global brands, including time spent working at a comScore-rated top 50 web property and two of the world's largest ad networks as Vice President of Marketing.

Rick develops and builds online media strategies for companies of all sizes, including several Fortune 500 companies. He has been quoted in and his companies profiled by CNBC Business, The Wall Street Journal, AMEX OpenForum, Portfolio, Law.com, Ars Technica, CBS MoneyWatch, and more.

He has also written for MediaPost, iMediaConnection, InsideCXM, and Ragan.

Rick also created the number one most-viewed banner of all time with over 3 billion impressions worldwide.

He blogs at RickRamos.com and is the founder of Rick Ramos Consulting.

What's Inside This Book?

This book is a reference book that was initially developed in a shorter form for my own content marketing needs but was fleshed out to be a more complete reference book.

It contains 365 short, less than a word or sentence concept, which is meant to get you thinking about new blog topics.

The ideas can be as simple as a single word that is meant to inspire or get you thinking. Hopefully, this will save you a few minutes or hours every month and help you overcome the occasional writers block.

Here are 10 examples:

1. New hire at the company
2. Trends you have noticed
3. Investor bios
4. New advertising campaigns
5. Tips for your prospective customers
6. Your local economy
7. Original internal research
8. Strategies to get things done
9. May 5 – Cinco de Mayo
10. Upcoming trade shows

14. Things you've learned to help you succeed

15. Your employees' goals

16. Where you see the industry headed

17. Trends you have noticed

18. Brainstorming ideas

19. Company photos

20. Interview someone internally

21. Top questions you receive from people about your business

22. What's your daily challenge?

23. What inspires you? Why?

24. What are your employees' plans for the future?

25. What's a day in the life of?

26. Who would you like to meet and why?

27. What's your favorite book?

28. What's your favorite quote?

29. Top 10 favorite employee YouTube videos

30. List of everyone's social media accounts

31. Get them to talk about their volunteer work

32. How you decorate your desk

Company Information

33. Securing new investors

34. Investor bios

35. Getting additional funding from current partners

36. Your business plan

37. How you handled a company crisis

38. Company logo history

39. Company tagline history

40. Getting a bank credit line

41. Job openings

42. Unique employee benefits

43. Your outside vendors

44. Your mission statement

45. Ethical standards of business

46. Internal memos

47. Show your charity work

48. Launching a new division

49. Innovation – what it means for your business

50. Corporate responsibility for the community

51. Teamwork in your business

52. Unique office art or decorations

53. Corporate governance

54. State of the industry

55. Buying another company

56. Launching another company

57. Why is your company different?

58. Marketing that is working for your company

59. New advertising campaigns

60. New marketing pieces

61. What are your company's future plans?

62. Sales method that is working for you

63. Your social media interactions

64. Myths and reality

65. Weird or unique office/factory sounds

66. Company milestones, such as the 1,000th widget sold

67. The early days of your company

68. Your original business plan

69. Company failures in the past

70. Company anniversary

71. Interview your investors

72. Funny events

73. Tradeshow floor interviews

74. Tips to use your product or service

75. What the public needs to know about your company

76. The many ways to reach someone at the company

77. Show behind the scenes

78. Create a contest

79. Create an award

80. Receive an award or form of recognition

81. Offer something free

82. Do a summary of your top blog posts

83. Speaking engagement for an employee

84. Information about lawsuits you've filed

85. Response to lawsuits filed against your company

86. Refuting false claims

87. Thanking people for saying positive things

88. Correcting misinformation

Your Customers

89. Tips for your prospective customers

90. Conversations with potential customers

91. Feature a customer's business

92. How your customers use your products

93. Inspirational thoughts from your customers

94. How they can increase their leads

95. How they can increase their sales

96. Ways to increase their profitability

97. Their social media presence

98. Their industry predictions

99. Trends they have noticed in their business

100. Review how you could help a potential customer

101. Reflection on client relations

102. Customer service

103. Quality issues voiced by your customers

104. Interview them

105. Issues you've addressed after a customer complaint

106. Best client of the year award

107. Q & A session

108. How can we help you?

109. What they need to know about a topic

110. What challenges do they face on a daily basis?

111. What are their goals?

112. "Ask us anything" column

113. How best to comment on your blog

114. Customer success stories

Global Economy

115. Overall global economic growth

116. Historical growth over time

117. Country-specific economic growth

118. Compare growth across different countries

119. Economic calculation of your products or services

120. Capital and rental costs

121. Opportunity costs analysis

122. Success and failure of the social system

123. Your local economy

124. Current news events that affect your industry

125. New laws that affect your industry

126. Laws that are being debated in Congress

127. Economic forecasts

128. Cultural issues you deal with

129. Geographic issues

130. Class warfare – rich versus poor

131. Your company's lobbying efforts

132. The real interest rates and effects on your industry

133. Futures and options use in your industry

134. Personal finance information

135. Corporate finance information

136. Tariffs and quotas

137. Monopolies in your industry – directly or indirectly

138. Paying cash versus barter

139. Fiscal policy

140. Country trade balances

141. The real exchange rate

142. Employment and unemployment

Research

143. Original internal research

144. Web analytic stats

145. Other companies' research

146. Education institution research

147. Social media surveys

148. Share survey results

149. Finding niches

150. Ask for feedback

151. Ask for photos of your product being used

152. Search terms people use to find your site

153. Ask an expert

154. Do a comparison test on a product or service

155. Get data and create an infographic

156. Market research about another industry that can indirectly affect your industry

157. Mathematical growth models

Psychological Issues

158. Success

159. Failures

160. How to move forward after a setback

161. Working as a team

162. Conflict resolution strategy

163. Things that are frustrating

164. Motivations

165. Gender issues

166. Creativity

167. Dealing with downtime

168. Vacation from the Internet

169. Strategies to get things done

170. Work/family balance

171. Letting things go

172. Having fun

173. Vacation ideas

174. Relaxation ideas

175. Communication techniques

176. Constructive criticism – giving and
     receiving

177. Passions

178. How did you become the person you
     are?

Holidays

179. Jan 1 – New Year's Day

180. Third Monday in January – Dr. Martin
     Luther King, Jr.

181. First January 20 following a presidential
     election – Inauguration Day

182. February 2 – Groundhog Day

183. February 14 – Valentine's Day

184. Third Monday in February – Presidents'
     Day / Washington's Birthday

185. February or March – Mardi Gras / Fat
     Tuesday

186. March 8 – International Women's Day

187. March 17 – Saint Patrick's Day

188. Sunday following full moon, March 22 to April 25 – Easter

189. April 1 – April Fools' Day

190. April 22 – Earth Day

191. May 5 – Cinco de Mayo

192. Second Sunday in May – Mother's Day

193. Last Monday in May – Memorial Day

194. June 14 – Flag Day

195. Third Sunday in June – Father's Day

196. July 4 – Independence Day

197. First Monday in September – Labor Day

198. September 11 – Patriot Day

199. September 17 – Constitution Day

200. Second Monday in October – Columbus Day

201. October 31 - Halloween

202. November 11 – Veterans Day

203. Fourth Thursday in November – Thanksgiving

204. December 7 – Pearl Harbor Day

205. December 25 – Christmas

206. December 26 through January 1 –
Kwanzaa

Birthdays

207. Customers

208. Famous people

209. Employees

210. Founder

211. Company birthday

212. Product birthday

Seasons

213. Start of spring

214. Spring cleaning – product cleaning

215. April showers

216. Fall

217. Leaves changing – company changes

218. Winter

219. Snow – staying indoors

220. Summer

221. It's hot outside

222. First summer job reflections

223. Family vacation

224. Company BBQ

Local Events

225. Sporting events

226. Outdoor festivals

227. Musical concerts

228. Art exhibits

229. Government meetings

230. Educational events

231. Food events

232. Fundraisers and benefits

233. Health events and fairs

234. Museums – new exhibits

235. Meetup.com

236. Picnics and parties

237. Pet shows – people love animals!

238. Religious and spiritual

239. Memorials

Industry Events

240. Upcoming trade shows

241. Summary of sessions

242. Interviews with industry people

243. Networking events

244. Photos of people you meet

245. What happened this week that can have consequences

246. Quote a speaker

247. Photos of all the booths

Memories

248. Dreams

249. Nightmares

250. Patents

251. School

252. Summer camp

253. Winning an award as a kid

254. Old toys

255. First crush

256. Different classes that affected you

257. Your first teacher

258. Your first work mentor

259. First day at school

260. Getting in trouble in school

261. Your best friend in elementary school

262. High school cliques

263. Your first computer

264. College

Entertainment

265. New industry books

266. Review a book

267. Get permission to post part of a book

268. Lessons learned from a book

269. New movies that feature your industry

270. A product in a movie from a customer or your company

271. Lesson from a movie that can be applied to business

272. How a movie character can use your product

273. TV shows about your business

274. Shows about the future and how business would change

275. Cartoons from your childhood

276. Fan fiction about a character working at your company

277. Fan fiction about a character reacting to your product

278. Songs that affect you

279. Songs that inspire

280. Songs to listen to at work

281. Song lyrics that teach

282. Sports teams you support

283. Athletes and business

284. Celebrity sponsor reactions

285. Post a quote from someone

286. Relate your business to a celebrity

287. Mention pop culture and how it relates

288. Get a local celebrity to do a Q & A

Memories

289. Advice from your parents when you were a kid

290. Advice from your friend when you were a kid

291. Something that affected you from childhood

292. Who was your idol and what did you learn?

Life

293. Tell a joke

294. Show your passion

295. Share your ups and downs

296. Talk about time savers

297. Share your "life hacks" to being more productive

298. What do you love most about your career?

299. What do you love most about your industry?

300. What's the most challenging part of your industry?

301. What I should have said

302. Signs of trouble

303. Keeping a secret

304. Something stupid you said and shouldn't have

Your Industry

305. Do's and don'ts of your industry

306. Perks of your industry

307. Quirks of your industry

308. How people view your industry

309. The reality of your industry

310. The press and how they speak about your industry

311. Tutorial on a topic of interest to your industry

312. Editorial news

313. Do a numbered list

314. Review something

315. Links to relevant content

316. Recommend a third-party solution

317. Industry controversy

318. List of industry experts

319. What makes your business special?

320. Talk about a popular post on social media

321. Disagree with a popular opinion

322. What's the latest trend?

323. Start a debate

324. Biggest industry blunders

325. Make some predictions

326. Share industry secrets

327. Expose an industry lie

328. Share an industry milestone

Technology

329. How technology affects your business

330. What technology empowers you?

331. Share what keywords bring people to your site

332. Moore's Law

333. The network effect

334. Futurists' predictions

335. The drop in processing costs

336. Cloud computing and its effect

337. Software as a Service (SAAS)

338. Industry technical architecture

News of the Weird

339. Weird social media rants from industry people

340. Arrests from people within your industry

341. Funny pictures from industry parties

342. Strange but true stories

Logistics, Manufacturing, and Development

343. How is your product made?

344. What are the materials?

345. Where is it created in the world?

346. Where are all the parts from?

347. What's the environmental impact of your product?

348. What software do you use in your business?

349. How does your product or service get delivered?

Marketing

350. New sale or discount

351. New reward or loyalty program

352. Special holiday promotion

353. New affiliate program

354. Customer referral program

355. New contest

356. Celebrity endorsements

357. New video product demonstration

358. New tutorials

359. New website

360. New social media page

361. Analysis of other companies' ads

362. Behind the scenes for your advertisements

363. An interview with your ad agency

364. Put a presentation on slideshare.net and post it on your blog

365. New brochure – put the PDF on the web or slideshare.net

WRITING POWER WORDS
BONUS CONTENT

Turn on the TV and put on a sensational news channel. You'll find that over the course of a few minutes, you'll experience a range of emotions. Now, notice the words they use to trigger these emotions. These are called "power words"; they can foster emotions quickly and make your writing more engaging. People are hardwired with specific emotions from birth: fear, comfort, greed, joy, lust, anger, and desire for the forbidden.

FEAR

1. Alarming

2. Affliction

3. Aftermath

4. Agony

5. Anguish

6. Annihilate

7. Apocalypse

8. Apprehension

9. Attack

10. Anxiety

11. Backlash

12. Battle

13. Beating

14. Beware

15. Blast

16. Blinded

17. Bloody

18. Catastrophic

19. Caution

20. Chilling

21. Collapse

22. Con

23. Consequences

24. Crazed

25. Crippling

26. Criticism

27. Crisis

28. Crush

29. Danger

30. Deadly

31. Death

32. Deception

33. Destroyed

34. Devastating

35. Disastrous

36. Disturbing

37. Distressful

38. Discomfort

39. Drowning

40. Dumb

41. Embarrass

42. Epidemic

43. Explosive

44. Exposed

45. Fail

46. Feeble

47. Fired

48. Fooled

49. Forewarned

50. Frenetic

51. Fraud

52. Frightening

53. Gambling

54. Gore

55. Gullible

56. Hack

57. Hazardous

58. Helpless

59. Hoax

60. Horrific

61. Hurt

62. Injured

63. Implications

64. Imprison

65. Invasion

66. Irresponsible

67. Jail

68. Jeopardy

69. Lawsuit

70. Lethal

71. Looming

72. Lunatic

73. Lurking

74. Massacre

75. Meltdown

76. Mired

77. Mislead

78. Mistake

79. Nightmare

80. Outbreak

81. Pain

82. Pale

83. Pandemic

84. Panic

85. Peril

86. Pitfall

87. Plague

88. Plummet

89. Plunge

90. Prey

91. Prison

92. Ramifications

93. Repercussions

94. Reckoning

95. Revenge

96. Rickety

97. Risky

98. Ruse

99. Scary

100. Scream

101. Searing

102. Shattering

103. Slaughter

104. Slave

105. Smash

106. Spine-tingling

107. Stupid

108. Suck

109. Suppress

110. Swindled

111. Target

112. Terrifying

113. Threatening

114. Toxic

115. Trick

116. Unstable

117. Unpredictable

118. Vaporize

119. Victim

120. Volatile

121. Vulnerable

122. Warning

123. Weak

124. Wobbling

Comfort

125. Accurate

126. Anonymous

127. Authentic

128. Backed

129. Best-selling

130. Cancel Anytime

131. Certified

132. Dependable

133. Endorsed

134. Expert

135. Free-Trial

136. Guaranteed

137. Genuine

138. Lifetime

139. Licensed

140. Money-back

141. Nameless

142. No Questions Asked

143. No Strings Attached

144. Official

145. Privacy

146. Proficient

147. Protected

148. Proven

149. Qualified

150. Recession-proof

151. Reliable

152. Refund

153. Research

154. Results

155. Secure

156. Specialist

157. Tested

158. Trustworthy

159. Try for free

160. Verified

161. Unconditional

162. Unidentified

163. Unsigned

164. Zero Obligation

165. Zero Risk

Greed

166. Affluence

167. Bargain

168. Bargain-basement

169. Best

170. Billion

171. Bonanza

172. Cash

173. Celebration

174. Concession

175. Deal

176. Deduction

177. Deluxe

178. Discount

179. Dollar

180. Double

181. Dough

182. Elite

183. Expensive

184. Extra

185. Feast

186. Finest

187. Fortune

188. Free

189. Freebie

190. Frenzy

191. Frugal

192. Gift

193. Giveaway

194. Goldmine

195. Greatest

196. Inexpensive

197. Jackpot

198. Lush

199. Luxurious

200. Markdown

201. Massive

202. Million

203. Money

204. Nest egg

205. Omit

206. Opulent

207. Preeminent

208. Prize

209. Profit

210. Prosperity

211. Rebate

212. Reduced

213. Reduction

214. Rich

215. Rock-bottom

216. Savings

217. Six-figure

218. Soaring

219. Steal

220. Sumptuous

221. Treasure

222. Triple

223. Unsurpassed

224. Well-appointed

225. Whopping

226. Windfall

227. Zero-Down

Joy

228. Amazing

229. Astonishing

230. Astounding

231. Belief

232. Blissful

233. Brave

234. Breathtaking

235. Cheer

236. Confidence

237. Conviction

238. Courage

239. Delightful

240. Daring

241. Defiance

242. Delight

243. Devoted

244. Excited

245. Eye-opening

246. Faith

247. Fearless

248. Fulfill

249. Grateful

250. Guts

251. Happy

252. Heart

253. Hero

254. Hope

255. Jubilee

256. Magic

257. Marvelous

258. Mind-blowing

259. Miracle

260. Pleasurable

261. Remarkable

262. Sensational

263. Spectacular

264. Spirit

265. Staggering

266. Stunning

267. Surprising

268. Triumph

269. Uplifting

270. Victorious

271. Wonderful

272. Wondrous

Lust

273. Audacious

274. Banned

275. Bold

276. Brash

277. Crave

278. Desire

279. Depraved

280. Dirty

281. Exposed

282. Forbidden

283. Lonely

284. Lust

285. Naked

286. Naughty

287. Provocative

288. Prohibited

289. Scandalous

290. Sensual

291. Shameless

292. Sinful

293. Sleazy

294. Sloth

295. Spank

296. Steamy

297. Sweaty

298. Tantalizing

299. Tawdry

300. Thrilling

301. Uncensored

Anger

302. Abused

303. Arrogant

304. Backstabbed

305. Battered

306. Bullshit

307. Coward

308. Crooked

309. Crush

310. Disgusting

311. Force-fed

312. Foul

313. Hate

314. Lies

315. Loathsome

316. Loser

317. Lying

318. Mistreated

319. Neglected

320. Obnoxious

321. Patronizing

322. Payback

323. Preposterous

324. Punish

325. Revolting

326. Ruthless

327. Smug

328. Snob

329. Snooty

330. Snotty

331. Terrorized

332. Underhanded

Desire for the Forbidden

333. Backdoor

334. Banned

335. Barred

336. Behind the Scenes

337. Black-Market

338. Blacklist

339. Bootleg

340. Censored

341. Concealed

342. Confessions

343. Confidential

344. Controversial

345. Covert

346. Covered

347. Disguised

348. Forbidden

349. Forgotten

350. Hidden

351. Illegal

352. Insider

353. Lost

354. Masked

355. Obscured

356. Outlawed

357. Pirate

358. Private

359. Secrets

360. Smuggled

361. Strange

362. Stolen

363. Suppressed

364. Unauthorized

365. Unlicensed

Excerpt from "Content Marketing: Insider's Secret to Online Sales & Lead Generation" for sale on Amazon.com at: http://amzn.to/10MY0fZ

Headlines That Get 1000% More Clicks

Excited to read this section? Yes, you should be! The headline for this section is enticing and hopefully makes you want to read what's in this section. Headlines are the first impression someone will get from your article and are many times the teaser that will be used to share something on social media. Readers generally pay attention to the title for two seconds and quickly decide if they want to read an article. You need to catch their interest quickly. Here are the elements of a good, catchy title:

Try and simplify your article to its core message.

Create a hook that gets people's attention.

Use your SEO keywords where possible.

So you might be asking, How do I create a good hook? Well, here are a few things you can try:

Make the reader curious – Using words like "shocking" or "secrets revealed" always work. Try and think of other teaser words that work with your piece.

Use numbers – "Increase your click-through rate over 5 times!"

Ask a question – Address who, what, when, where, how and why. ("When to quit your job" or "Why your diet might be hurting you," for example.)

Use the formula = Number (Reasons/Ways) (to/why) _____.

Just fill in the formula and you can usually come up with a decent headline.

("5 reasons why content marketing works," for example.)

Just always try and make sure that your headlines match the content. Also try and keep a similar tone when possible on a headline. You don't want to be funny and cute with a headline when discussing something very serious in an article.

More Books by Rick Ramos

"Content Marketing: Insider's Secret to Online Sales & Lead Generation"

http://amzn.to/10MY0fZ

"How to Blog: 72 Tips for Big Success" (FREE)
http://www.rickramos.com